KV-388-532

The harvest mouse
weaves a straw nest
in the corn

The emperor penguin's chick
keeps off the cold ice by
sitting on its parent's feet

4

A tree frog with
only a cradle of foam
to keep her eggs moist

The finished nest
of the weaver bird

5

Copyright © 1979, 1983 by Grisewood & Dempsey Ltd.

Published in this edition by Galley Press, an
imprint of W. H. Smith and Son Limited,
Registered No. 237811 England.

Trading as WHS Distributors, St John's House,
East Street, Leicester, LE1 6NE.

ISBN 0 86136 930 0

All rights reserved. No part of this publication
may be reproduced, stored in a retrieval
system, or transmitted in any form or by
any means, electronic, mechanical, photocopying,
recording or otherwise, without prior written
permission from the publishers.

Printed in Italy by Vallardi Industrie Grafiche, Milan.

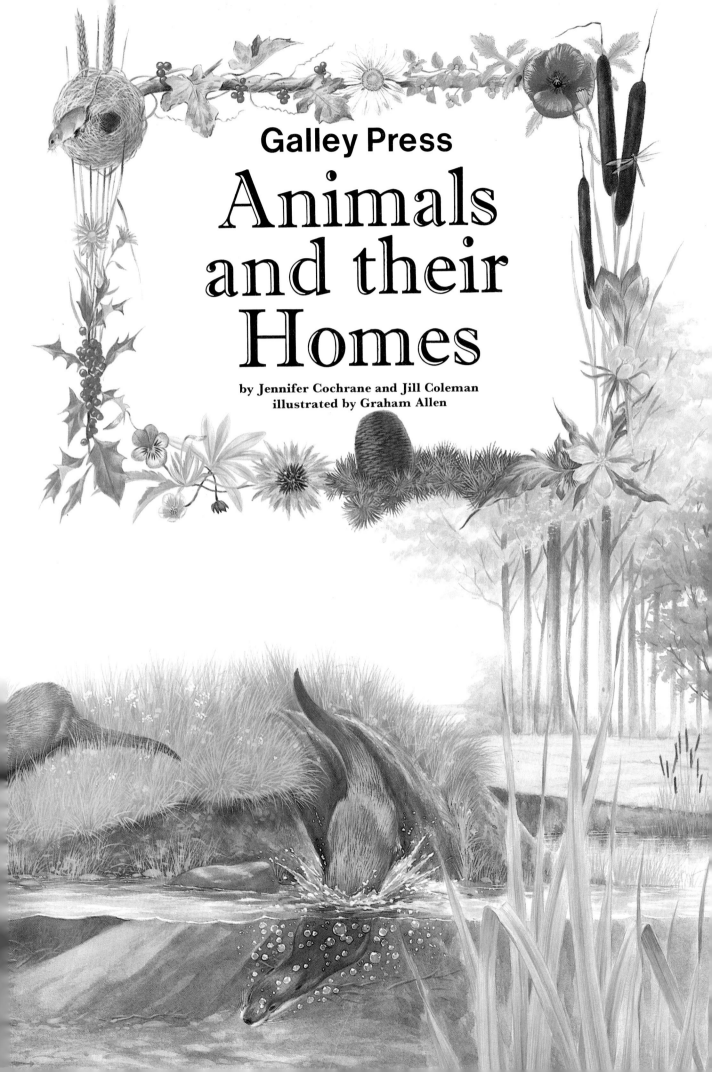

Galley Press

Animals and their Homes

by Jennifer Cochrane and Jill Coleman
illustrated by Graham Allen

Homes for babies and bad weather

ONLY a few animals build homes where they live from year to year. Most live in the open and find or build a home only when it is time to bring up a family or seek shelter from winter weather.

Field voles normally sleep in a burrow under the ground. But, for her babies, the mother vole plaits a soft, round nest of grass and stems, well hidden from hungry enemies.

The stickleback is an unusually fine father, for a fish. He collects waterweeds and forms them into a tunnel-shaped nest. The female lays her eggs and leaves the male to guard them.

Tropical forests are warm and damp. There is so much
water in the air that frogs can live high in the trees
with only the steamy air to keep their skins moist.
But frogs' eggs need water. So, when it is time to
breed, the blacksmith frog comes down from the trees.
He finds a pool and makes his nest – a private pool
within a pool. Piling mud on mud, he builds up a
round wall, high enough to keep out hungry fishes.
Then he sits in the pool and calls for a mate.
Once his call is answered and the eggs are laid,
the two frogs go back to the treetops, leaving
their eggs to hatch, safe in the watery nest.

One tiny creature who never sees the holly at
Christmas is the dormouse. This sleepy
mouse climbs into his straw nest at the first
breath of winter and settles down to sleep.
Even if you pick him up you will not
disturb his deep slumber: But do
not try to wake him; he may die
if he is taken from his bed.

A hidden town beneath the prairies

IT is morning on the American prairies. The sun has just risen and the dew is drying on the grass. Already a bison is grazing and a ferret is looking for prey. His nose twitches as he smells the prairie dogs and creeps towards them. The family of prairie dogs have long been awake, collecting grass for their breakfast.

At the entrance to their burrow, stands the oldest male in the family, keeping watch for enemies. Suddenly he sees the ferret and barks a warning to his family. The loud yelp brings them running back to the burrow. Only when they are safely underground does he leave his post and dive down to safety.

The family burrow has an entrance shaft from the surface which leads into several other tunnels. At the end of each tunnel is a sleeping chamber. So many other families have burrows nearby that together they make a huge underground town of connecting tunnels.

On the surface, the only signs of the prairie dogs' town are the mounds of earth piled up around the entrances to the burrows. These mounds are used as look-out posts, and also stop rainwater from flooding the tunnels.

More homes under the ground

MANY small animals have homes under the ground where they are safe from larger enemies and the cold weather.

The mole spends almost all his life burrowing through the ground, in search of juicy worms to eat. He scrapes out the earth as he goes and pushes it behind him with his strong front paws. Every so often he turns and pushes the loose soil to the surface. It piles up on the surface in little heaps, called molehills. The mole's nest is in a dark hole, stuffed with dry leaves, at the end of a tunnel.

Rabbits also have underground homes. Several families live together in a 'warren'. Each rabbit has its own burrow which is joined to the rest by a tunnel. Baby rabbits live in a secret burrow lined with grass and fur. Only their mother knows where they are.

These badgers have been living in their 'set'
for a long time. But they are always improving
it, digging new burrows and bringing in new
grass and leaves to sleep on. During the day
they stay underground, but when it is dark they
come out to find worms and small animals to eat.

In spring a fox moved in to one of their empty
burrows to have her cubs. Now the cubs are
nearly full grown and will soon leave home, but
the mother will stay in the burrow for winter.

Compared with the badgers' neat set, the fox's
home is dirty and untidy. The badgers take all
their rubbish to a special dump, away from the
set. But the fox never clears out the old bones
and rubbish that litter her burrow. The badgers
do not like the smell. So they have blocked
the tunnel that joins her home to theirs.

Safe shelters for eggs and nestlings

MOST birds do not need homes all year round. It is safer for them to fly from place to place. But they need a safe place to lay their eggs and look after their young. The type of nest a bird builds depends on where it lives and what kind of bird it is. The longer the baby bird takes to grow up, the better the nest must be.

The robin lives in gardens and hedgerows. It builds a small cup-shaped nest of grass and twigs. This robin has found a warm, sheltered spot in an old shoe.

The oven bird lives in South America. Its nest is made of small lumps of clay, squashed together. It looks like an old-fashioned baker's oven. Sometimes the birds have to leave their nests because the hot sun turns them into real ovens.

House martins live in mud nests under the roofs of houses. They help each other to fetch lumps of mud, and stick them together into cup-shaped nests.

The golden oriole weaves a grass hammock between two branches.

The woodpecker chips a hole in a tree trunk with its hard beak. The hole is just big enough for the female to squeeze in and lay her eggs.

The bittern's nest is just above the water. It is built from reeds woven together.

The tailor bird stitches two leaves together to make a bag for its eggs.

The weaver bird uses its feet and beak to weave a basket-like nest. Sometimes hundreds of nests hang like giant fruits from one tree.

A stranger in the nest

AFTER laying her eggs, the reed warbler flutters away to find food, before settling down to hatch them. But leaving the nest is risky because there is a thief about. The cuckoo cannot build her own nest so she must steal a home for the egg she is about to lay; and the reed warbler's tidy nest is perfect.

Quickly the cuckoo swoops on the unguarded nest, and lays her egg. Then she takes up one of the warbler's eggs from its mossy bed and drops it, smash, on the ground.

When the reed warbler comes back, she does not notice that a different egg is in her nest. She sits on all the eggs to keep them warm and free from danger. She does not know that the worst danger is in her nest.

Before her own eggs are ready, the cuckoo egg cracks open. The baby cuckoo is pink and bald, but very strong. As soon as the reed warbler flies off to feed, it sets about destroying her unhatched chicks. It wriggles under each egg in turn and heaves it out of the nest. Now the reed warbler will have only one gaping mouth to fill.

Every moment is taken up fetching caterpillars and other insects. Every day the greedy nestling grows; first too big for the nest, then so big that the reed warbler has to perch on its back to feed it. Soon it will be strong enough to fly away to its winter home in Africa, and the tired little reed warbler will be able to rest.

Master craftsmen at work on the river

THE beaver protects itself from hungry bears and mountain lions by building its home in water. A family of beavers share a home and they all help to build it. They are expert carpenters.

The family need a deep, still pool to build their home in. Sometimes they are lucky and find one. But often they have to make a pool in a river. They do this by building a wall of sticks and mud across the river.

They need a lot of wood to make the wall, so they cut down the nearby trees by chiselling through the trunks with their sharp front teeth. Then they drag the branches into the river.

The wall, or dam, is made of strong branches, pushed deep into the river bed, with thinner sticks woven in between. The gaps are filled with mud and stones so the water cannot flow through. It collects in a deep pool, just right for the beavers' home.

In the middle of the pool, they make a pile of branches, so tall that it sticks up above the water. Then they gnaw underwater tunnels into it.

At the end of the tunnels they chew out a big room to live in. The room is above the water so it is dry. The beavers cover the outside of the pile with mud and reeds to stop the cold and water getting in, but they leave a hole in the top for air.

The finished home is called a lodge. But even when it is complete the beavers' work is not over. The beaver family in the picture built their lodge three years ago, but they have a lot of work, apart from repairs, to do before winter comes.

When the river freezes over, they will not be able to leave their pool to find food. So they are making a big pile of tender young branches near their lodge. When they are trapped under the ice, they will have a store of their favourite food to nibble on until spring comes.

Two clever nest builders

SOME of the strangest animals in the world have their homes in Australia. One of the oddest is the platypus. Its body is furry, but it has webbed feet and a beak like a duck. And unlike other furry animals, it lays eggs.

The platypus lives near water. When it is time to lay her eggs, the female prepares the nursery. It is a nest of soft reeds at the end of a long tunnel above the water. The tunnel is blocked up with mounds of soil which she has moulded with her tail. They keep the nest warm and stop other animals from getting in. She stays in the nest, curled up around her eggs until they hatch.

from Australia

The rat kangaroo on the opposite page looks like a very small kangaroo. It has strong back feet for hopping and a pouch on its belly to carry its babies in. It cannot carry anything with its front paws, so it uses its long flexible tail like an arm.

To build its nest, it scratches out a hollow in the ground near a tree or bush. Then it piles grass into neat bundles, picks the bundles up with its tail and carries them to the hollow. When there is enough grass, it pats it into place with its tail and the nest is ready.

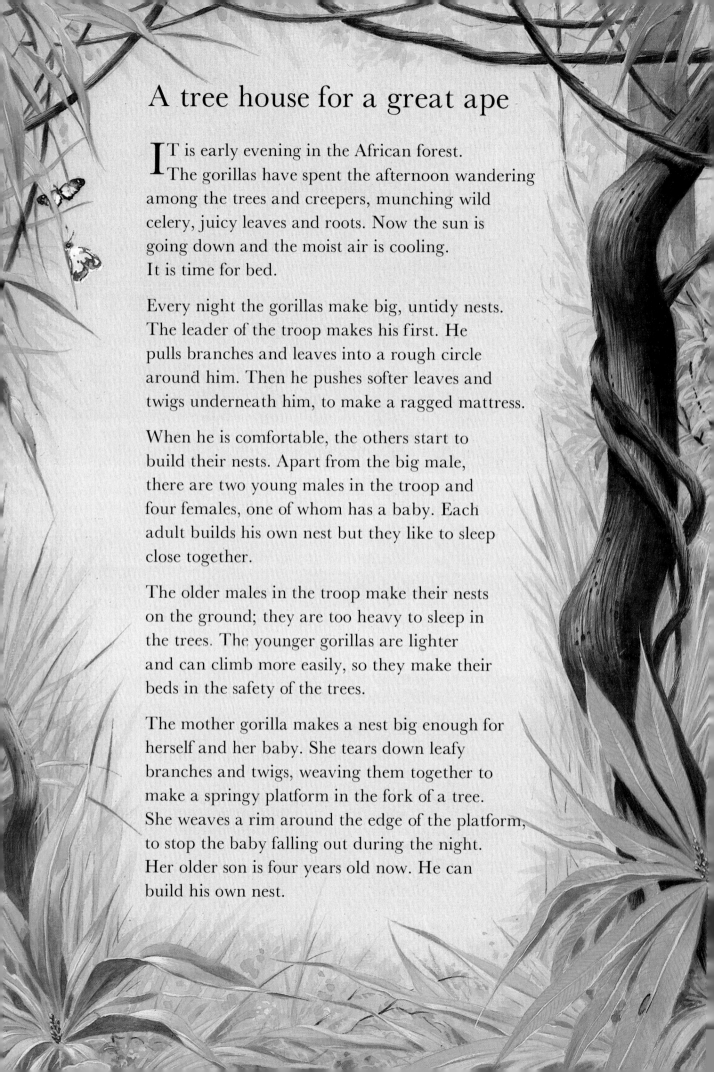

A tree house for a great ape

IT is early evening in the African forest. The gorillas have spent the afternoon wandering among the trees and creepers, munching wild celery, juicy leaves and roots. Now the sun is going down and the moist air is cooling. It is time for bed.

Every night the gorillas make big, untidy nests. The leader of the troop makes his first. He pulls branches and leaves into a rough circle around him. Then he pushes softer leaves and twigs underneath him, to make a ragged mattress.

When he is comfortable, the others start to build their nests. Apart from the big male, there are two young males in the troop and four females, one of whom has a baby. Each adult builds his own nest but they like to sleep close together.

The older males in the troop make their nests on the ground; they are too heavy to sleep in the trees. The younger gorillas are lighter and can climb more easily, so they make their beds in the safety of the trees.

The mother gorilla makes a nest big enough for herself and her baby. She tears down leafy branches and twigs, weaving them together to make a springy platform in the fork of a tree. She weaves a rim around the edge of the platform, to stop the baby falling out during the night. Her older son is four years old now. He can build his own nest.

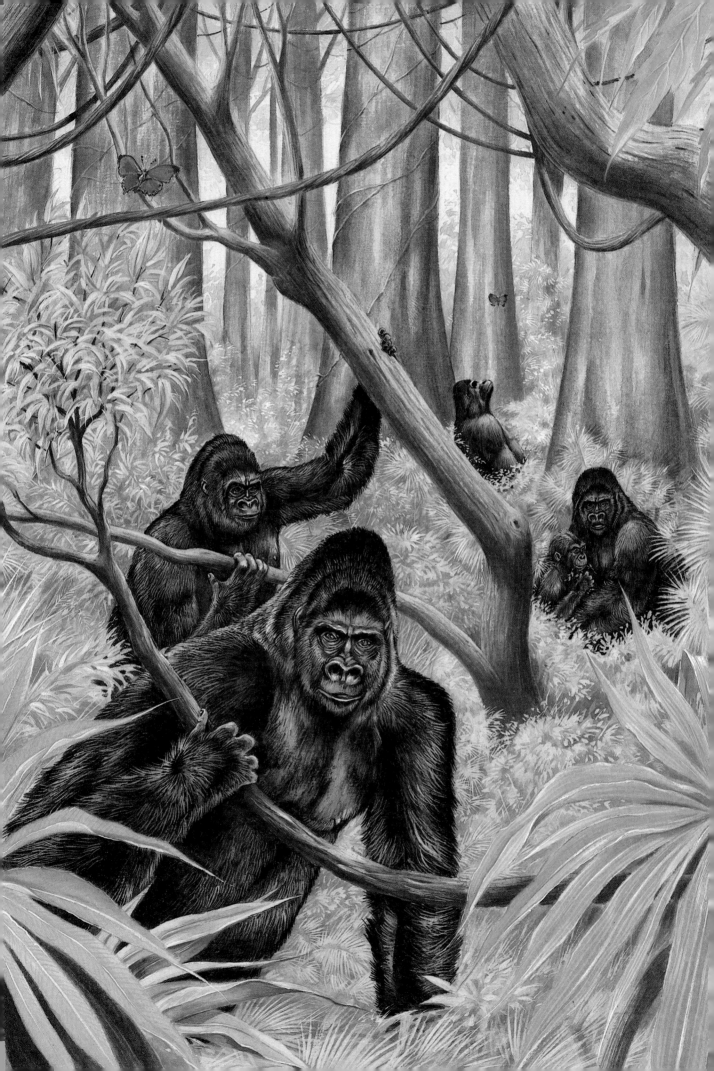

A winter drey to be proud of

HIGH above the ground, a sudden gust of wind shakes the branches of the pine trees. The pine needles rustle and cones drop to the ground. The squirrels cling tightly to the swaying branches, then return to their shrill chattering. It is a busy time for them; they are getting ready for winter.

Until now the three young squirrels, born in spring, have been living with their mother. Their nursery was a ball of twigs lined with warm fur. But now they are too big to live together. They must build their own dreys before the cold weather comes.

One of the young ones has already finished his drey and the others have come to look. The older squirrels take no notice; they are busy gnawing pine cones and chasing butterflies.

The young squirrel's drey is a big untidy ball in the fork of a tree. It is woven of twigs, strips of bark and the remains of an old crow's nest. There is no entrance; the squirrel will have to push his way in through the tangled sticks and close the hole after him. Inside the drey he has made a lining of grass and moss.

As well as building dreys, all the squirrels are eating as much as they can. When the frosts come, there will be very little food and they will not want to leave their warm winter homes. They are also burying any cones and seeds they cannot eat. These will stay fresh in the cold ground ready for the squirrels to dig up later.

Hard workers in a sunny meadow

IT is a hot, lazy summer afternoon. Most of the animals are dozing in the shade, but the bumblebees are hard at work. They buzz from flower to flower, sucking up nectar with their long tongues and combing the pollen which collects on their furry bodies into 'pollen baskets' on their legs. They will take the pollen and nectar back to their nest to feed the hungry babies.

The bees' nest is an empty vole's burrow, lined with dry grass and leaves. On the floor of the nest are the egg 'cells' containing the bee grubs.

The cells are little wax cups, moulded by the bees from wax made in their bodies. The queen bee lays an egg in each cup, and the other bees, called workers, put a store of nectar and pollen in with the eggs.

The eggs grow into wriggly, white grubs which eat all the nectar and pollen in their cells and grow and grow. When they are big enough, they spin a long thread of silk and wind it around themselves to make a soft cocoon. When they come out of the cocoon they will be full-grown worker bees, ready to make egg cells and fetch food for the next batch of hungry grubs.

The city of the workers

THE ants' city is a mound of earth in a hidden corner of the meadow. It is a crowded, bustling place. The ants swarm up the sides of the mound and scurry along the tunnels inside, each busy with its own special task.

All summer, the ant queen has been laying her eggs in a dark tunnel at the bottom of the mound. The eggs grow into hungry grubs which spin silk cocoons around themselves and then turn into ants.

The worker ants sort the eggs, grubs and cocoons into separate piles and put them into tunnels where they will be warm and safe. The baby ants

are helpless, so the workers feed and protect them. They have done their work well this summer; so many new ants have been born that there is not enough room for them all. The workers have to make the city bigger.

So they dig new tunnels deep into the soil under the mound. A troop of ants work together, scraping the earth away with their strong jaws. When the tunnels are finished there will be even more work to do. Old tunnels will have to be repaired and a fresh cover of leaves and grass must be put over the top of the mound to keep the inside of the city warm.

The ants will be busy until winter. Then they will sleep in deep tunnels at the bottom of their city until the warm weather wakes them up to start building again.

Small creatures with the skill of craftsmen

SOME of the most elegant homes are built by animals so tiny that we hardly notice them.

Weaver ants sew leaves together to make a nest. They use the silk spun by their larvae for thread.

Leaf cutter ants eat a special type of fungus which they grow on 'farms' in their nest. The fungus grows on leaves chewed up by the ants. It grows nowhere else, so when the queen starts a new nest she takes some of the fungus with her.

The water spider weaves an underwater web between two plants. When the spider plunges into the water, tiny bubbles stick to hairs on its body. These bubbles get trapped under the web and join up to make one big bubble. The spider can stay under water for a long time, breathing the air locked in its web.

Termites live together in huge mounds of earth baked hard by the sun. In the centre of the mound is the royal chamber where the king and queen termites live. The queen does nothing but lay eggs all day. She and her mate are looked after by the worker termites. Often termite mounds are taller than a man.

The caddis fly larva is a soft helpless grub. It builds a hard case around its body to protect itself from hungry enemies. The case is made from bits of dead plants, or stones and grains of sand. These are stuck on to a silk tube which the larva weaves around its body. Enemies cannot see the disguised grub, lying among the stones and sand at the bottom of the pond.

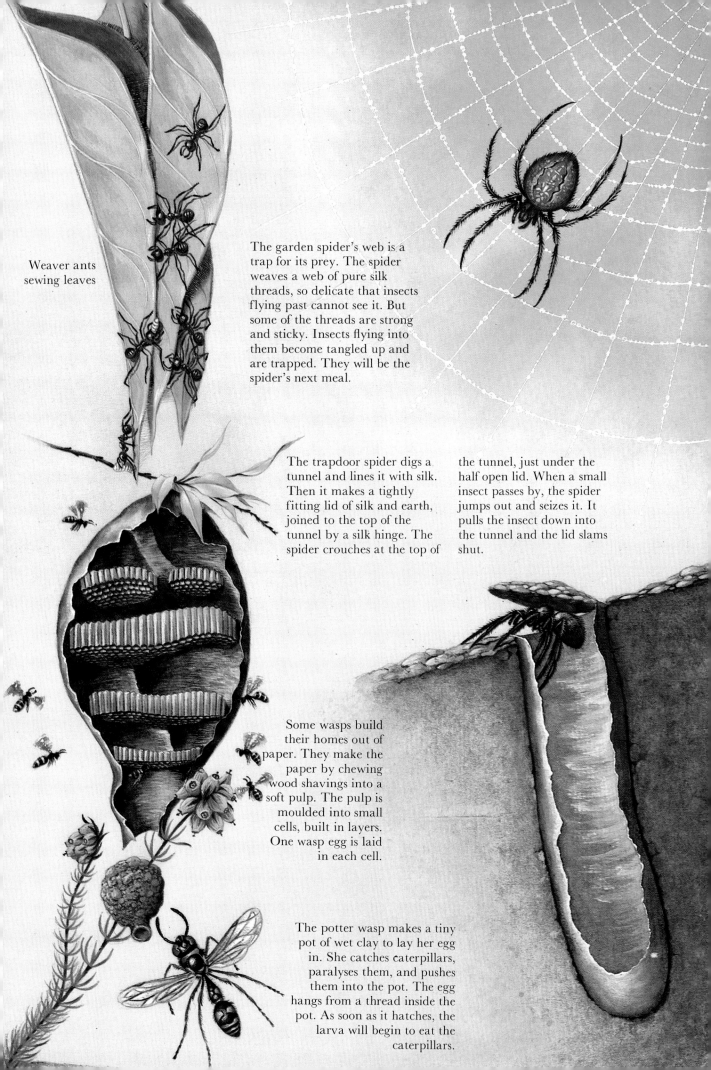

Weaver ants
sewing leaves

The garden spider's web is a
trap for its prey. The spider
weaves a web of pure silk
threads, so delicate that insects
flying past cannot see it. But
some of the threads are strong
and sticky. Insects flying into
them become tangled up and
are trapped. They will be the
spider's next meal.

The trapdoor spider digs a
tunnel and lines it with silk.
Then it makes a tightly
fitting lid of silk and earth,
joined to the top of the
tunnel by a silk hinge. The
spider crouches at the top of

the tunnel, just under the
half open lid. When a small
insect passes by, the spider
jumps out and seizes it. It
pulls the insect down into
the tunnel and the lid slams
shut.

Some wasps build
their homes out of
paper. They make the
paper by chewing
wood shavings into a
soft pulp. The pulp is
moulded into small
cells, built in layers.
One wasp egg is laid
in each cell.

The potter wasp makes a tiny
pot of wet clay to lay her egg
in. She catches caterpillars,
paralyses them, and pushes
them into the pot. The egg
hangs from a thread inside the
pot. As soon as it hatches, the
larva will begin to eat the
caterpillars.

Follow the weaver bird as it makes its nest

An orb web spider on its web

1

2

3

A wheatear at the entrance to its burrow

A goldcrest in its nest

A hermit crab inside the snail shell it borrows for its home